# William
# SHAKESPEARE

WHO WAS...

# William
# SHAKESPEARE

*The mystery of the
world's greatest
playwright*

## RUPERT CHRISTIANSEN

✳ **SHORT BOOKS**

Published in 2004 by
Short Books
15 Highbury Terrace
London N5 1UP

10 9 8 7 6 5 4 3

A CIP catalogue record for this book
is available from the British Library.

ISBN 1-904095-81-X

Printed in Great Britain by
Bookmarque Ltd, Croydon, Surrey

For Harry Shearer, Eliza Chubb, Freddy Le Fanu,
Alfie MacGibbon, John Phipps, Nat Philipps –
and Ferdy Saumarez-Smith

Who was William Shakespeare?

You might think that's a silly question: everybody knows about William Shakespeare, don't they? Ask your parents or teacher, and they will tell you that he is the most famous playwright in the world. He lived in Stratford-upon-Avon during the time of Queen Elizabeth I and wrote *Hamlet*,

*Romeo and Juliet*, *Macbeth*, *A Midsummer Night's Dream*, *Henry V* as well as many other plays and poems. Every day, several of these plays are performed somewhere in the world. Tens of thousands of books have been written about them, and they have been turned into over three hundred film versions. Tap the name 'Shakespeare' into a search engine on the internet and the number of references which come up – millions of them – is mind-boggling.

But William Shakespeare is a Mystery Man – one of the greatest mysteries in history. We don't know for certain that he actually wrote the plays that go under his name. Almost nothing survives from his lifetime four hundred and fifty years ago to tell us what sort of person he was, who his friends were or what he looked like. None of his letters or his belongings survive either.

We don't even know how he spelled his surname

– it appears on various documents as Shackspeare, Shakspere, Shake-Speare, Shacksper, Shackspeere, Shakespea, Shagsper, Shaxberrd, Shakxpere and Shackespe. It's true that Elizabethans just didn't care much about spelling, but all these different names have made some people think that the man usually called William Shakespeare and born in Stratford-upon-Avon in 1564 may not have been the same person who wrote all those brilliant plays and poems.

Let's play detective and look at the evidence. Then you can make your own mind up and answer the question: who was William Shakespeare?

\*\*\*\*\*

In Elizabethan days, Stratford-upon-Avon was a fairly ordinary and peaceful sort of a place. About a thousand people lived and worked there, and their greatest fear was the plague – a disease spread by fleas nesting in the fur of the black rats which scuttled about in the thatch or between the wattle-and-daub walls of everybody's houses. The plague was a terrible disease. It produced revolting squelchy boils all over your body before reducing you to screaming agony, and in the summer that William Shakespeare was born, an outbreak in Stratford killed one in every fifteen people.

William's family escaped this horror. They were much like other families, really, and lived in a reasonably spacious and comfortable house in the middle of town which you can still visit to-day. William's father John bought and sold wool skins and leather hides, which he also made into gloves, belts and purses. We don't know much more about him, because although he could probably read perfectly well, he never learnt to write so much as his own name. (On official documents, he signed with a wiggly **X**). John's wife Mary came from a nearby village and gave birth to eight babies – it was quite common in those days to have as many children as that. Four of them died before they grew up; the ones who survived were called Joan, Gilbert, Edmund and William.

At first John Shakespeare was quite successful. One year, he was even elected mayor of Stratford. Sadly, when William was about ten, he made some criminal, under-the-counter money dealings, and was found out. Stratford put him in disgrace, and from then on the family had to struggle. Young William probably helped his father in his workshop and would have watched the hot, sweaty and stinky business of stripping and boiling the skins and hides.

He also had to go to school, of course. It sounds a good deal more boring than it is now, and nobody today could stand for a minute the bum-numbing routine that boys as young as eight suffered (girls, lucky things, didn't go to school at all, but learnt their lessons at home). Classes started at six in the morning and finished at six in the evening. You sat on hard benches, and everyone had to stand up and bow whenever the teacher entered or left the room. Pens were made by dipping the sharpened tips of feathers, known as quills, into bottles of ink (and it was considered extremely good fun to gather these quills by pulling a bag over a goose's head and sending it into such a blind spin of panic that it flapped its wings until the feathers fell off).

Most of the day was spent in saying prayers or repeating the rules of Latin – the language which you had to use if you wanted to speak out loud in class. Everything had to be learnt off by heart, and anyone who made bad mistakes or dared to misbehave in even the smallest way would be given an immediate thrashing. There were no sports, no outings, just lessons, lessons, lessons, and more Latin, Latin, Latin. Ugh.

Sunday was the only day off, but Sunday meant church – and not just for an hour, but for most of the day. People who didn't turn up were severely punished. 'A fart of one's arse for you!' screamed one mad old woman in Stratford when she was punished for skiving off with a ducking in the river.

In those times, following the laws of Christianity was compulsory – you couldn't choose what to believe, and the nations of Europe were either Catholic or Protestant. Protestants hated Catholics, Catholics hated Protestants; they fought bloody wars against each other. England was then a Protestant nation, and Catholics were burnt at the stake; France and Spain were Catholic countries and they treated Protestants in just the same way. William would have thought that the mad old woman was possessed by the devil and shuddered to think that unless she repented, she was bound for the eternal tortures of hell when she died.

It wasn't all bad. In some ways, children then had a lot more freedom than they do now. There was time in the summer evenings to race off with your friends and spend hours fishing the streams or playing with bows and arrows in the country-side around the town. There was a sort of football which the boys enjoyed too – it didn't have many rules, and would get quite wild as the ball (made from the bladder of a pig) was kicked through the streets. Even more riotous were the special days at Christmas and harvest time in the autumn when everyone was allowed to say and do exactly what they pleased, turning the whole town into one great street party of crazy games and practical jokes. Throwing bags of flour over the vicar and the schoolmaster, setting off fireworks in the middle of the night, and sticking your head up a lady's skirt were usually deeds that were severely punished. On these rare riotous occasions, however, everyone just laughed.

But for 350 days of the year, it wasn't a life with much fun in it. You could only eat whatever grew on the farms around Stratford, and if the crops were ruined by bad weather, everyone went hungry. Water came from a bucket carried from a well. Apart from the plague, there were all sorts of diseases for which there was no cure or treatment, and most people could expect to die before they were forty! No cars, of course, no gas or electricity, no flushing loos or running baths, no police. No newspapers or magazines either, though pedlars travelled on foot around the country selling sheets printed with songs which explained the great events of the time. Otherwise you only heard what was going on in London or abroad from what travellers passing along the rough, muddy tracks told you.

Among those travellers were troops of strolling players. When they came to town on their carts, which they turned into open-air stages, everyone got very excited because there was no television or cinema and the players' colourful costumes and extravagant language would have seemed very strange and interesting. Once, when William was eleven, there was even a great pageant in the park around the castle of Kenilworth near Stratford – Queen Elizabeth I was visiting, and she was honoured with a show full of special effects and fireworks – rather like what happened during Queen Elizabeth II's Golden Jubilee. People came from miles around to watch and never forgot the glory of it all. Events like these must have first got William Shakespeare interested in the theatre.

John Shakespeare's money troubles meant that William would have no chance to go to university, when he left school at fifteen. How did he spend the following years? Perhaps he helped his father, perhaps he became an infants' schoolteacher, perhaps he worked for a lawyer, perhaps he was caught poaching deer from a nobleman's estate near Stratford and had to leave town quickly to avoid arrest and trial. There are all sorts of stories and legends, but nobody knows which of them is true, and it's unlikely that we ever shall.

All we know for certain – because huge dusty old books recorded all the births, weddings and deaths in Stratford – is that when he was eighteen, William married a local girl called Anne Hathaway who was already pregnant by him. They had three children, first Susanna, and then the twins

Hamnet and Judith. One day, a band of players called the Queen's Men came to Stratford, with their star performer, a clown whose name was Richard Tarlton. In the town that the players had visited just before, a disaster had occurred: one of the actors had been accidentally killed in a tavern brawl, and they were now one short. Did William offer his services, seizing the chance to become a glamorous actor and escape from his young family and the dull small-town life of Stratford? Let's imagine that he did, and from there made his way to – LONDON!

\*\*\*\*\*

It wasn't anything like the city we know today; for one thing it was much, much smaller. Today there are something like fifteen million people living in London – four hundred years ago there were about 200,000, and many parts which we now think of as central – Islington, Hampstead, Ealing, Wimbledon or Clapham, for example – were quiet little villages surrounded by fields.

Elizabethan London was all situated within a mile or so of the river Thames, whose rough black waters were dense, day and night, with long barges and little rowing boats called wherries, which richer folk used like taxis. The roadways were little more than dirt tracks, sodden with mud in winter, dusty and hard in summer and constantly blocked with horse-drawn wagons, coaches and carts. There was only one bridge, London Bridge, and both sides of it were lined with higgledy-piggledy houses, shops, market stalls and even a church. Just to cheer everyone up and remind them to keep on the right side of the law, the bleeding chopped-off heads of traitors were displayed on spikes stuck above the bridge's gateway.

Yes, London had many splendours. There were abbeys and cathedrals and churches, there were grand mansion houses ranged along the river banks. The outside of wealthy people's houses were richly coloured and their clothes elaborately jewelled and decorated. The Queen and her court and parliament resided at the magnificent palaces of Westminster and Whitehall; the Tower of London was a high-security fortress and prison, where weapons and treasures were stored, coins forged – and torture and execution carried out.

But how would you like to live somewhere with no traffic control or police? A place without any proper system of collecting rubbish or flushing away sewage, so that what we would dump in the loo or the dustbin was simply thrown out of the window? A place where the rotting corpses of dead horses, cats and dogs were left lying in the streets for rats to feed off? Imagine the stink.

Such things made London a filthy, noisy chaos, full of 'a great number of dissolute, loose and insolent people', all jostling and elbowing each other, with worse manners and language than a crowd at a football match. The taverns were full of fighting and brawling and stabbing; pickpockets, thieves and beggars were even more of a menace than muggers are nowadays.

For all that, it was a terrifically exciting place for a young man full of energy and ambition. What sights there were to see, what money to make, what people to meet, what stories to hear, what pleasures and entertainments unheard of in Stratford-upon-Avon – from the cruel sports of bear-baiting and cock-fighting to the smoking (in clay pipes) of tobacco leaves, newly imported from the mysterious, still unexplored lands of America. Another new wonder of London were the theatres or playhouses. The very first one was built in 1567, only three years after Shakespeare was born (before then, actors had simply travelled around the whole time like circus folk, setting up a stage wherever they could find an audience). These new theatres did not have roofs, and their stages were open platforms, covered only with a canopy. Built from wood, they were painted in gorgeous colours. The only advertising was a flag, which flew from the top of the building on the day a show was being played. Performances were generally held in the afternoon over the spring and summer, and they were packed out with as many as two or three thousand people.

Inside you could either stand on the ground floor (in which case you were called a 'groundling') or sit on hard benches (bring your own cushions) in one of the terraced balconies. Audiences were rowdy and restless, and the actors had to speak out loud and clear to command attention. There was no popcorn or Coke in those days, but people ate hazelnuts and drank ale while they were watching – if the actors were no good, people would throw bits and pieces or shout rude comments at them.

Although there was almost no scenery, costumes were lavish and there was a lot of noise and action. Trumpets brayed, drums thundered and productions were full of elaborate dances, exciting duels and spectacular processions. There was hardly a minute's boredom – and if there was, the audience wouldn't hesitate to start booing and hissing.

All this meant that to be involved in the theatre you needed to be pretty tough and thick-skinned. There were no colleges or courses to teach acting – you got taken on at fourteen or fifteen as an apprentice or 'hireling' and worked your way up from boring backstage jobs to one-line parts to big starring roles. Some actors did become very famous and made a lot of money, but for most of them it was a rough, hard life, very violent and quarrelsome.

It was also quite demanding. When the companies weren't playing in London, they were touring the country, with all the stresses and strains of constant travelling. There were thousands of lines to learn (parts were written out by hand on long scrolls), because as many as thirty plays were performed in rotation every year. You could be fined one shilling for being late for rehearsal (that would be about £25 today), three shillings if you weren't in costume in time for the show, ten shillings if you were drunk before a show and £1 if you forgot to turn up at all.

Unless you were a religious fanatic who didn't approve of people enjoying themselves, everyone from the Queen and her courtiers to the poorest tapster or scullion loved to visit the theatre. But that didn't mean that there was much respect for actors – the law assumed they were little better than crooks and classified them alongside beggars and tramps, so it wasn't the sort of profession that parents would have wanted their children to enter.

Two odd things about Elizabethan theatre. The first is that, because it was considered indecent for women to act on the stage, all the roles for ladies and girls were played by teenage boys wearing dresses and wigs. In those days, their voices didn't break until they were sixteen or seventeen, so it was more convincing than you might think. The second is that plays were almost always written in a mixture of ordinary, everyday language and richly elaborate poetry which is often quite difficult to understand when you read it on the page. In the theatre, it all makes sense: this poetry is usually spoken by grand or royal or romantic characters, and when the actors are good, the words ring out and seem to fill the theatre, almost as though they are singing.

Anyway, let's imagine that young Will Shakespeare joined one of these companies of actors, and over the next three or four years learnt the craft of acting and all the business of putting on a show. He never became an absolutely brilliant actor and was probably best at playing old men and country bumpkins rather than princes or heroes. This was just as well, as all the companies were desperate to draw the crowds with exciting new plays and because he wasn't learning other people's lines every day, Shakespeare had some time in which to write them.

Shakespeare's plays were immediate big hits. He wrote four about the bloody Wars of the Roses – with characters like Joan of Arc and the hunchback Richard III – and a very, very gory one about a Roman general called Titus Andronicus who ends up taking revenge on a woman he hates by baking the blood and bones of her murdered sons into a pie and making her eat it! It wasn't all horror. Young Shakespeare also wrote two very funny plays: *The Taming of the Shrew*, about a girl who is determined not to have a boyfriend, and *The Comedy of Errors*, about identical twins who get into a terrible muddle.

These plays were so successful that other people in the theatre business began to get jealous of Shakespeare. Who on earth did he think he was? He hadn't been to university, he was only a jumped-up idiot from a little out-of-the-way place called Stratford-upon-Avon. Somebody wrote that he was 'an upstart crow', but Shakespeare wisely didn't answer back. That seems to have been typical of him: most people who knew Shakespeare seemed to have liked him well enough, but he kept himself to himself and stayed out of trouble. After he died, one friend of his, another playwright called Ben Jonson, wrote: 'I loved the man and do honour his memory... he was indeed honest and of an open and free nature; had an excellent phantasy, brave notions and gentle expressions, wherein he flowed with that facility, that sometime it was necessary he should be stopped.' In other words, he was a very nice chap, but he never stopped talking.

I like to think of Shakespeare as a rather nervous and excitable fellow. Sometimes he would be tremendously warm and friendly, and deeply interested in listening to what you had to say, but then he'd suddenly run off for no reason in the middle of a conversation, and then you wouldn't see him for weeks. You couldn't help liking him, even though you never felt you knew him.

But that's just what I imagine.

My other guess is that Shakespeare didn't spend a lot of time in London. Instead he went home to his wife and children in Stratford, where he could write without being disturbed. He certainly didn't buy any property in London – he always rented rooms in friends' houses instead. But it's an odd thing that nobody in Stratford seems to have known that he was an actor or a playwright. Did he keep it a secret, and if so why?

Another mystery is what Shakespeare did next. In the boiling hot summer of 1593, there was a terrible outbreak of the plague in London. Flea-infested rats scuttered and scatted under floorboards and behind wainscots, infecting as many as a thousand people a week with the deadly disease. Everything in the city closed down, including the theatres. Did this drive Shakespeare back to Stratford? Did he travel to France and Italy? Or did he perhaps stay in the magnificent palace in Titchfield in Hampshire, owned by a handsome young nobleman called Henry Wriotheseley (pronounced 'Rose-lee', believe it or not), the Earl of Southampton, to whom he was very distantly related? The Earl liked the company of writers and other clever people, who enjoyed his lavish free hospitality often for months at a time. In return, they entertained the Earl and paid him special compliments – Shakespeare, for instance, dedicated two long poems called *Venus and Adonis* and *The Rape of Lucretia* to him.

At Titchfield, Shakespeare would have met for the first time in his life a collection of very glamorous, sophisticated and aristocratic figures who liked nothing better than to sit around talking about poetry. Shakespeare might have fallen in love with one of the beautiful women of Titchfield, and he certainly wrote some lovely short poems called 'sonnets' to 'a dark lady' with whom he was very smitten. (Poor Anne, stuck in Stratford with her three small children.) To be honest, we do not know for sure whether Shakespeare went to Titchfield at all, but we shall hear more about Henry Wriotheseley later in this book.

Even if life was relaxing and luxurious at Titchfield, Shakespeare would have been keen to get back to London and the theatre. Late in 1594, the plague died down and the playhouses were allowed to reopen. Shakespeare now wrote, in quick succession, three of his most beautiful plays – *A Midsummer Night's Dream* (that's the one with Bottom and the fairies; it's like a pantomime and it's the Shakespeare play that children enjoy most), *Romeo and Juliet* and *Richard II* – and he began to earn quite a lot of money. £250 a year may not sound like much to us today, when footballers and pop stars earn that much in an hour, but in Elizabeth I's reign it was a lot – at least ten times what a schoolteacher would earn.

What did he do with his money? On the whole, he was careful with it – remember that his father had got into trouble ten years earlier, so Shakespeare probably had to help him out with his debts. But he did make one big purchase: for the sum of £120, he bought the second largest house in Stratford. It was called New Place, and although the building was demolished in 1759, you can still walk round the gardens. We know from a drawing that its front was sixty feet long and seventy feet deep, and that it had three storeys, a courtyard and ten fireplaces. Several servants, and probably some older members of Shakespeare's or Anne's family, would have lived there too. At the same time, Shakespeare applied to officials in London for a coat of arms – a badge which confirmed to everybody that he was ranked in society as someone to be looked up to and respected, a gentleman and a landowner.

The coat of arms looks like this: you don't have to be a genius to notice that it contains a SPEAR and a falcon SHAKING its wings. It would have hung on a plaque above the front gate of New Place, as well as in prominent places in the main rooms. The motto, 'Non sanz droict' is old-fashioned French for 'Not without right' ('non sans droit'), and it means something like 'I only do something if I know that right is on my side'.

\*\*\*\*\*

Most of Shakespeare's early plays were presented at a theatre called – guess what? – The Theatre. It stood in a part of East London called Shoreditch and was rented out to Shakespeare's company.

When the agreement with the owner, Mr Giles Allen, came to an end, there was a huge quarrel. Mr Allen wanted to put the rent up, the actors refused to pay. The owner claimed he owned the building as well as the land; the actors claimed that he just owned the land. Eventually, the actors did something absolutely wicked.

One cold night over Christmas, while the owner Mr Allen was out of town, they armed themselves with swords and axes and pulled the theatre to pieces, loaded all the planks of wood into wagons and dragged them across the ice of the frozen Thames. There, on some rough land on the river at Blackfriars, they used all the timber to erect a new theatre which they called the Globe – a word that was hugely popular during an age which saw whole oceans and continents being explored by the likes of Sir John Hawkyns and Sir Francis Drake.

The most amazing thing about the actors'

daring scheme is that because of some Elizabethan property laws, the actors did actually have 'right on their side'. Mr Allen came back and not surprisingly flew into a rage. He sued for £800 of damages, including forty shillings for trampling down the grass. How dare the actors behave like that, he wrote to the Queen's court, 'pulling, breaking and throwing down in very outrageous, violent and riotous sort, to the great disturbance and terrifying not only of your subjects, said servants and farmers, but of divers others of your Majesty's loving subjects there near inhabiting'. All sorts of legal arguments ensued, but poor fuming Mr Allen never got his money back.

Its walls painted in sumptuous colours, the Globe was splendid and gorgeous and thrilling beyond any other theatre in London and the crowds flocked in their thousands to see the plays there. Shakespeare, who owned a tenth of the

Globe and therefore took a share of the profits, was inspired to write stirring dramas like *Henry V* (about the battle of Agincourt) and *Julius Caesar* (about the murder of the famous Roman general) and amusing comedies like *Much Ado about Nothing*, *As You Like It* and *Twelfth Night*. Once every month or so the company would be commanded to leave the Globe to perform their latest hit indoors, by candlelight, for the benefit of the royal court. There's even a story that the Queen so much enjoyed watching the escapades of the fat cowardly knight Sir John Falstaff, a character in Shakespeare's two plays about King Henry IV, that she told him to write something which showed him falling in love – the result being *The Merry Wives of Windsor*, another of his really funny comedies.

*****

After a long and glorious reign during which England became one of the greatest nations in Europe, Queen Elizabeth died in 1603. Because she had had no children, she was succeeded by her distant cousin, King James VI of Scotland, son of Elizabeth's old enemy Mary Queen of Scots. People's mood changed: there was much anxiety about the future, and fears as to what sort of a king James might prove.

Shakespeare seems to have become gloomier too. First he wrote some quite strange and bitter plays, like *Measure for Measure* and *Troilus and Cressida*. These are full of twisted angry characters, and as you watch them, you feel you can smell something rotten in the air, as though Shakespeare thought the whole world had turned nasty.

Then he wrote a series of dark tragedies – plays in which men who could be noble warriors or great leaders are destroyed both by a terrible situation and some fault in their personality. Prince Hamlet is commanded by a ghost to take revenge on the man who murdered his father, but can't find a way to take the right action. Old King Lear decides to abdicate his throne and divide his kingdom between his daughters: two of them turn against him and throw him out into a terrible storm, where he goes mad.

The Roman general Antony is so in love with the Egyptian queen Cleopatra that he loses an important battle. The ambitious Macbeth falls under the influence of some witches who inspire him to murder the king of Scotland and take the throne himself. Macbeth's enemies declare war against him and he is killed in a battle. (This play was written to please James I, whose ancestors had won that battle.)

*Hamlet*, *King Lear*, *Antony and Cleopatra* and *Macbeth* are reckoned to be among the greatest plays ever written – which seems like the right moment to ask the question: why does everyone think Shakespeare is so good? What is it that keeps him remembered four hundred years after he died? There were plenty of other playwrights in Elizabethan London, after all.

Here are some reasons why. First, Shakespeare was brilliant at telling stories. Within minutes, something exciting happens in every play – war breaks out, a murder is committed, ghosts appear, magic spells are cast, there's a bitter argument or a dirty rotten trick – which leaves you longing to know WHAT WILL HAPPEN NEXT.

Second, the plays are full of real and interesting people. Shakespeare had an amazing ability to get under everybody's skin and imagine WHAT IT

FEELS LIKE TO BE THEM. He understood what makes us all good or evil, sad or happy, brave or cowardly, why some succeed and others fail, and everywhere you go, you meet people who remind you of melancholy Hamlet or scheming Lady Macbeth, fat Falstaff or bumptious Bottom. And when something ghastly happens in life – a person you love is dying, there's a terrible quarrel between members of a family, there are fires and riots and people start killing each other – it's Shakespeare who seems to understand what goes on inside your head.

Another thing: in the plays, you never know quite whose side Shakespeare is on. When you watch a stupid soap show on the telly, you soon know who is nice and who is nasty – there are no surprises. But Shakespeare's plays aren't like that. Even if he was writing about Hitler or Osama Bin Laden, he would want to understand why they did the terrible things that they did. Nobody in Shakespeare's world is either totally evil or totally perfect, completely right or completely wrong – and that makes them very interesting.

Third, nobody has ever used the English language with more power than Shakespeare did. Like a great soccer player dribbling and bending and heading the ball, he can make words do anything and go anywhere. The plays and poems show that he had a vocabulary of over 25,000 words, about three times as many as most people.

Nearly two thousand of these words had never been written down before Shakespeare's plays – 'blanket', 'gossip', 'assassination', 'champion' and 'generous' are just a few of them. Some of these words have been completely forgotten today – I doubt you have ever heard anyone saying '**trundle tail**', '**fustilarian**', '**turlygood**' '**linsey-woolsey**', '**drumble**' or '**gorbellied**'\*, for example – and sometimes his poetry is so splendid and complicated that it is difficult even for English teachers to follow (although they probably pretend they can). But he also invented hundreds of simple phrases which people still use in ordinary conversation: 'in my mind's eye', 'we have seen better days', 'a pound of flesh' 'the wheel is come full circle', 'as good luck would have it', or 'murder most foul', for instance.

Perhaps Shakespeare's single most famous lines of all are 'Romeo, Romeo, wherefore art thou Romeo?' (from *Romeo and Juliet*) and 'To be or not to be, that is the question' (from *Hamlet*). Neither means quite what you might think.

'O Romeo, Romeo, wherefore art thou Romeo?'

---

\* '**trundle-tail**' – a long-tailed dog; '**fustilarian**' – an idiot; '**turlygood**' – a beggar; '**linsey–woolsey**' – rubbish; '**fustilarian**' – an idiot; '**drumble**' – sluggish; '**gorbellied**' – hugely fat is spoken by the young girl Juliet as she comes out on to her balcony, after a ball at which she has fallen in love with the handsome young Romeo. 'Wherefore?' does not mean '*where*?' but '*why*?' – O Romeo, Romeo, *why* are you called Romeo? She wishes he was called something else, because Romeo is the name that belongs to the family of Montagues, who have a terrible feud with her own family the Capulets, and by falling in love with him, she is falling in love with the enemy. So let's forget about our names and our families, she says to herself...

O Romeo, Romeo, wherefore art thou Romeo?
Deny thy father and refuse thy name,
Or if thou wilt not, be but sworn my love
And I'll no longer be a Capulet

'To be or not to be, that is the question' is

spoken by Prince Hamlet. He has just seen and spoken to the ghost of his murdered father the King, and this ghost orders Hamlet as a loyal son to take revenge on the man who killed him – Hamlet's uncle Claudius, who has married Hamlet's widowed mother. Hamlet is left in a state of shock. He feels he must obey the ghost, but at the same time, can't face up to the dreadful responsibility. He is so depressed that he thinks about committing suicide.

'To be or not to be' means 'Is it worth living, or isn't it?' And then he wonders whether it is better just to sit and suffer whatever problems life throws at you – or to fight back and attempt to sort them out…

To be or not to be; that is the question:
Whether 'tis nobler in the mind to suffer
The slings and arrows of outrageous fortune,

Or to take arms against a sea of troubles,

And, by opposing, end them.

*****

Shakespeare and the company of actors at the Globe became one of London's top attractions, and by 1608, they had enough money to buy a smaller indoor theatre called the Blackfriars, where they could show plays during the winter months, when the open-air Globe was unusable.

The Blackfriars was quite smart and plush and expensive – in fact, you needed at least sixpence to get in (admission at the Globe, you may remember, could cost as little as one penny). There was no standing room, everyone had a seat, and the stage was lit with hundreds of candles. In the

Globe, because there was so little scenery, the audience had to use its imagination a lot; in the Blackfriars, there were more possibilities. You could change the number of candles and create the effects of darkness and light; you could conjure up tricks and illusions; you could roll spectacular pieces of scenery down from the ceiling; and you didn't have to shout the whole time to make yourself heard.

All this changed the way Shakespeare wrote. One of his very last plays, *The Tempest,* opens with a terrific storm and a shipwreck. The action then takes place on a magical island. One of the characters, Ariel, flies on and off the stage like Peter Pan, a banqueting table vanishes underground, and the goddess Juno descends from the roof. An audience which had never seen a film or a computer game would have been amazed, and a special performance of the play was given as part of the celebrations surrounding the wedding of James I's daughter.

After writing *The Tempest*, Shakespeare seems to have lost interest in the theatre. We don't know why. Perhaps he felt it was time to stop when the Globe burnt down after a cannon was fired by mistake into its thatched roof (it was rebuilt a year later, with tiles); perhaps he was just getting old. He returned to live in Stratford, where he devoted himself to looking after his business and property interests, and nobody in the town ever mentioned the fact that he was a famous playwright.

What about Shakespeare's children? His son Hamnet had died young, just before *Hamlet* was written. His daughter Judith married a wine merchant; his daughter Susana married a doctor called John Hall.

Hall kept a diary, recording the treatments he gave his patients, and they make you feel sick. The medicines he used weren't the pills and injections we have today, but weird potions and lotions, made from things like spiders' webs, radishes and syrup of violets. One day his wife had terrible indigestion, which Dr Hall cured by pouring a cup of hot white wine into her bottom. It 'brought forth a great deal of wind', he wrote in his records, 'and freed her from all pain.'

Shakespeare died in 1616. He was just 52 years old, which in those days was quite a good old age. On the floor near the altar of Holy Trinity church in Stratford is a small flagstone. You can still see it – and local legend relates that Shakespeare's body was buried underneath. The flagstone is engraved, in capital letters and old-fashioned spelling, with these creepy lines:

GOOD FREND FOR JESUS SAKE FORBEARE,
TO DIGG THE DUST ENCLOASED HEARE:

BLESTE BY YE MAN YT SPARES THES STONES,
AND CURST BE HE YT MOVES MY BONES.

This is a warning: 'Good friend, I beg you not to dig up what is buried underneath. Blessed be the man who leaves this stone untouched; Cursed be anyone who moves my bones.' Not surprisingly, nobody has ever dared lift the stone to see what lies underneath.

Shakespeare's will has his very shaky signature on it, and must have been written when he was already very ill (we don't know what disease he died from). He left most of his money and property to his daughters and their families. He gave £10 (not a great deal) to the poor of Stratford, and some money for three of his old theatre friends to buy rings to wear in his memory. To his widow Anne, he left only his 'second-best bed with the furniture'. But this isn't quite as cruel as it might seem. John and Susana Hall came to live in New Place, and what this probably means is that Anne had to give up the main bedroom to them and move into a smaller one.

And that was the end of William Shakespeare of Stratford-upon-Avon. As I mentioned at the beginning, none of his books, belongings, clothes or letters survive to fill in the gaps in the picture. The world's greatest playwright was also the Elizabethans' greatest Mystery Man.

Shakespeare has no direct descendants. His wife Anne died in 1623, his daughters Susana in 1649 and Judith in 1662. Judith's children died before they had children of their own; Susana's daughter Elizabeth died childless in 1670. Gradually everything about William Shakespeare was lost or forgotten, and although stories went round about him – some said he had been a schoolmaster, some said he had been caught poaching deer on an estate near Stratford and that's why he left London – nobody really knew if they were true or not. But what did survive was a book, published in the same year that Anne died. It is called *Mr. William Shakespeares Comedies, Histories & Tragedies*; it contains 907 pages and the words of 36 plays, and it is one of the most important books in the history of the world.

*****

For the last two hundred years, people have tried to fill the gaps in the story of the Elizabethan Mystery Man, but until we can travel back in time, we shall never know the truth about William Shakespeare for sure.Here are some of the problems which confront the Shakespeare detectives:Why did people of the time say so little about him? There are very few documents with his name on them, and no hand-written manuscripts of the plays. Even the six examples of his signature look different, as though they might be faked. You'd think that someone so successful for such a long time would have been discussed by everyone in their letters, but hardly anyone ever describes or even mentions him. And why did absolutely nobody in Stratford seem to know that he was a famous playwright? Shakespeare's plays are full of references to France and Italy, to Ancient Greece and Rome and to fine points of the law. How did a boy educated at a local grammar school, who never went to university and probably never travelled abroad, come to know so much? Where did Shakespeare spend the ten years between leaving school and becoming a playwright? Why is his grave unmarked by a name? Is it his grave at all? The more questions you ask, the flimsier the evidence becomes, and everything melts down to two big questions:

DID WILLIAM SHAKESPEARE FROM STRATFORD-UPON-AVON WRITE ALL THOSE PLAYS? AND IF HE DIDN'T, THEN WHO ON EARTH DID?

*****

Let's look at the different theories. Then you can make up your own mind.

**Francis Bacon** was a very learned lawyer, politician, historian and writer. He was so brilliant, in fact, that he was sent to Cambridge University when he was twelve, and soon started complaining that nobody there could teach him anything! He directed plays for his friends when he was a student and wrote some (not very good) poetry. He was also close to Shakespeare's playwright friend Ben Jonson.

But what makes him so interesting to the Shakespeare detectives is that he loved devising 'cryptograms'. These are messages in code, where the words look quite normal on the page, but which actually contain secret information if you know the key. For example, read only the first word in every line of a poem – or change every 'a' into an 'e', and every 's' into a 't' – and a sentence will emerge. But cryptograms are much more com-plicated than that. They were used a lot in Elizabethan times by politicians who wanted to get secrets through to their spies in France and Spain – England's enemies – when they were wor-ried that letters might be intercepted.

Bacon always wanted to be a playwright, but his father persuaded him to become a lawyer and politician instead. This meant he was much too busy and important to write plays – in any case, suppose the Queen or one of her ministers took offence at one of his characters or stories? Some people think that he secretly offered the actor William Shakespeare money if he would allow Bacon to use his name and pretend that he had written Bacon's plays. Did Shakespeare agree, and never tell anyone what he was doing?

The Shakespeare detectives have combed their way through the plays trying to find cryptograms which Bacon might have slipped into Shakespeare's plays as hidden evidence that he was their real author, but the only ones that have ever been discovered are totally idiotic. One is a line which reads 'Shakst spur never wrote a word of them', and which you can only find by matching letters alongside words beginning with letters from Bacon's name. The other is the anagram of 'honorificabilitudinatibus', a very long nonsense word (like 'supercalifragilisticexpialidocious') which occurs in a play of Shakespeare's called *Love's Labour's Lost*. One detective noticed that this word contained the anagram of 'Franiiiiii Bacon'. Why six 'i's? Because 'Fransix' sounds like 'Francis', especially if you are French and pronounce it 'Franceez'. Why this should mean that Francis Bacon wrote Shakespeare's plays, I can't imagine.

**Edward de Vere, Earl of Oxford.** This is an idea first put forward eighty years ago by a schoolmaster called Mr J. Thomas Looney. He thought that Shakespeare's plays were written by the Earl of Oxford, a nobleman who, like Francis Bacon, did not want to be publicly known as a writer. Looney noticed in some old documents that the Earl was every year paid the huge sum of £1,000 by the Queen. But the documents do not say why he was paid this money, and Looney guessed that it must be a payment for secretly writing propaganda plays which would support the Tudor dynasty.

What proof did he offer? A line in *Romeo and Juliet* which reads 'I am a candle-holder'. Another Elizabethan word for candle-holder is 'trestle', and the Earl of Oxford's grandmother was called Elizabeth Tressell. So the line is code for 'I am one of the Tressell family'. Please, Mr Looney – his granny? One line out of hundreds of thousands? You call that proof?

The Earl of Oxford died in 1604, twelve years before William Shakespeare. Even this inconvenient fact did not put Mr Looney off: Oh well, he said, all the plays that Shakespeare is supposed to have written after 1604 were actually written by the Earl of Oxford before he died and just kept in a drawer until the actors were ready to perform them! One more thing, added Mr Looney – the lion on the Earl of Oxford's coat of arms is holding, or even shaking, a spear. So he must be Shakespeare! He must be, he must be!

Well, the man's name was Looney, so what more can you expect?

*(This is a paragraph strictly for people with a very silly sense of humour. There is one little story about the Earl of Oxford, nothing to do with Shakespeare, which might amuse you. 'This Earle', someone wrote later in the seventeenth century, 'making his low obeisance to Queen Elizabeth, happened to let out a fart, at which he was so abashed and ashamed that he went to travell, 7 yeares. On his returne, the Queen welcomed him home, and sayd, My Lord, I had forgott the Fart.')*

**Christopher Marlowe.** This one is more interesting. Marlowe was a poor shoemaker's son from Canterbury, born in 1564, the same year as Shakespeare. He was astonishingly clever and won a scholarship to Cambridge University. Halfway through his course, he left England suddenly and went to France, setting himself up in Rheims as a student Catholic priest – in fact, he was working as a secret agent for the English government, spying on revolutionaries thought to be plotting against Queen Elizabeth!

Later he returned to London, where he was involved in a nasty street brawl which ended up with someone being killed. Luckily for Marlowe, there wasn't enough evidence to bring a guilty conviction, so he was let off. Then, in the late 1580s, before the name of Shakespeare was well known, he became a successful writer of rather violent and gruesome plays like *Doctor Faustus*, the story of a man who sells his soul to the devil. There is no evidence that he ever met Shakespeare, but it would be amazing if two such famous playwrights, working in the same city at the same time, didn't know each other.

The Shakespeare detectives believe that Marlowe also had another life, mixing with rough and sinister types in the criminal underworld, as well as working as a secret agent. In 1593, he got into big trouble. Leaflets were appearing round London, criticising the Queen's government and expressing views about God and the Christian religion that were strictly against the laws of Elizabethan England. Anyone found guilty of those offences could only expect to be executed, after days of appalling torture.

Another playwright called Thomas Kyd was suspected of being their author, but when he was arrested, Kyd claimed that Marlowe was responsible (which he probably was). Marlowe was summoned for questioning before the dreaded Court of the Star Chamber, but as in the case of the brawl, there wasn't enough evidence to charge him, so he was released. Then other witnesses against Marlowe appeared, and the order went out to arrest him again for further questioning. Things were getting very hot indeed.

That very day, however, Marlowe met up with three rough characters – Nicholas Skeres, Robert Poley and Ingram Friser. They spent several hours drinking together, and after supper, there was a tremendous argument over who should pay the bill.

Eventually, the enraged Marlowe attacked Friser with a dagger. Friser grabbed Marlowe's hand and drove the dagger straight though his skull above his right eye, killing him at once. Friser was arrested, but later released, on the grounds that he had been defending himself. Or so the story went.

The Shakespeare detectives have different ideas: what they think really happened is this. Marlowe had a close friend, Thomas Walsingham, who was connected to the Secret Service, but he wasn't altogether a good guy, and had broken the law in ways that Marlowe knew about. Worried that Marlowe might spill the beans and betray him if he was tortured, Walsingham decided that Marlowe could be useful to him in Europe, spying on Catholics plotting against Protestant England. He would be even more useful if everyone thought he was dead.

So the Shakespeare detectives think that Walsingham staged Marlowe's death – it was all faked, like a play. Poley, Skeres and Frizer were in fact Walsingham's agents, busy doing his dirty work for him. The person murdered wasn't Marlowe at all, but some poor kidnapped wretch whose blood-stained corpse was quickly bundled into a coffin, with no questions asked – such things were easily done.

Marlowe, meanwhile – so the theory goes – escaped to Europe. And for the next twenty years he lived on under another name and continued both his spying and his play-writing, having bribed his friend the actor William Shakespeare to let him use his name. Perhaps he even sent Shakespeare the manuscripts, and paid Shakespeare to copy them out in his own handwriting. This would explain why Shakespeare kept so mysteriously quiet about everything to do with his writing, and why nobody seemed to know much about him. He was Marlowe's frontman, but he didn't want any awkward questions asked. Convinced?

About fifty years ago, an American Shakespeare detective called Calvin Hoffman got permission to open the Walsingham family tomb in the church of

St Nicholas in Chislehurst, Kent. Hoffman hoped that it would contain manuscripts which would prove that Marlowe was the true author of Shakespeare's plays. But all he found was sand.

Still convinced?

**The Sonnets.** This is the biggest mystery of all, and the Shakespeare detectives have offered hundreds of different explanations of it.

In 1609, a book containing 154 short poems (and one long one) was published by Mr Thomas Thorpe. It was entitled *Shake-Speares Sonnets*. A sonnet, by the way, is the name given to a certain type of love poem which is only fourteen lines long. Most people think that Shakespeare had written them about fifteen years earlier (when he was at Titchfield with the Earl of Southampton), and there are so many printing mistakes that most people think that Shakespeare didn't know anything about the book – in those days, you could get away with that sort of thing.

On the first page, these strange words appear:

TO.THE.ONLY.BEGETTER.OF.

THESE.ENSUING.SONNETS.

Mr.W.H.ALL.HAPPINESS.

AND.THAT.ETERNITY.

PROMISED.

BY.

OUR.EVER-LIVING.POET.

WISHETH.

THE.WELL-WISHING.

ADVENTURER. IN.

SETTING.FORTH.


T. T.


What on earth does this mean? T. T. are the

initials of Thomas Thorpe, but do those initials sitting at the bottom of the page, like a signature, mean that he wrote the words above them? Putting full stops after every word is confusing. 'Wisheth the well-wishing adventurer in setting forth' simply isn't proper English. Were some words left out? According to my dictionary, to 'beget' something means to give birth to it. Does 'only begetter' mean the person who actually wrote the sonnets, or the person who inspired the poet to write them? Is T. T. the 'only begetter'? And who the blazes is 'Mr W. H.'? Why not 'Mr W. S.'? Perhaps it was meant to be 'Mr W. S.', and the 'H.' is just a mistake made by the printer. Or Mr W. SH.?

The Shakespeare detectives have puzzled over this for months and years, and nobody has come to any satisfactory conclusion. Mr W. H. – hmm. Could he be Henry Wriotheseley, the Earl of

Southampton, with his initials reversed for secrecy? But why should he have wanted his identity kept secret? Then there was another earl whom Shakespeare might have known called William Herbert, the Earl of Pembroke. Was he Mr W. H.? But why call him plain Mr if he's an Earl? In Elizabethan times, anyone who dedicated a book to a nobleman would always do so with far more fuss and flourish – calling him my noble Lord, and claiming to be your humble servant – that sort of thing. Or was Mr W. H. Henry Wriotheseley's stepfather William Harvey? Or Shakespeare's brother-in-law, William Hathaway?

Here are some of the other theories. The family of Edward de Vere, Earl of Oxford, had as a motto for its heraldic shield the Latin phrase 'Nil vero verius' (which means 'nothing is more true than truth'). This is (almost) an anagram of 'OUR.EVER-LIVING' and could therefore imply that the Earl wrote the Sonnets. It is certainly odd to describe someone still alive as 'ever-living' – it's an adjective you'd normally use of someone who was dead and 'living for ever' in heaven. The Earl of Oxford had died in 1604, five years before the Sonnets were published. And there are some lines in one of the sonnets (number 76, to be precise) which are also very suspicious:

Why write I all still one, ever the same,
And keep invention in a noted weed,
That every word doth almost tell my name

'Ever' in the first line is an anagram of 'Vere'; a 'weed' is a disguise; and an anagram of 'every word' doth almost spell... – Oh, all right, 'Eyword Ver' isn't quite Edward de Vere, but it's close enough to be fishy in a line which is strongly hinting at something.

But the strangest explanation of all is that Mr W. H. is Mr William Hall ('*Mr W.H.ALL.*HAPPINESS') – which was Shakespeare's code name. And why did he have a code name? Because he too was a spy, mixed up with Walsingham and Marlowe. Your evidence, please? In 1596, old government records show that William Hall and William Wayte were both paid £15 for carrying secret messages to the Netherlands. The following year, another old document mentions that William Wayte (the same man?) started a lawsuit against William Shakespeare. Four years later, a William Hall is known to have travelled to Denmark, perhaps on another secret mission. And what play, set in Denmark, is thought to have been written in that very same year? Shakespeare's *Hamlet*! Surely it's just another strange coincidence...

*****

Before there were scientific tests for forgery (nowadays we can tell how old paper is, for example), many crooks tried to fake Shakespeare's manuscripts and then make money by selling them. Most of these frauds were soon uncovered, but one young man in the late 18th century had extraordinary success. His name was William Henry Ireland, the nineteen-year-old son of a London bookseller. He started by tracing over pictures of Shakespeare's signature and then bought a stock of crusty and yellowing parchment paper and mixing old recipes for ink.

He then announced that an elderly man who lived in a country house had given these ancient manuscripts to him before he died. There were hundreds and hundreds of sheets – whole plays called *William the Conqueror* and *Vortigern and*

*Rowena*, letters from Shakespeare to his wife Anne and Queen Elizabeth, even a complete list of all the books in Shakespeare's library.

All of them complete fakes! But the newspapers were full of the great discovery and William Ireland was suddenly the centre of attention. It's impossible to imagine how anybody could have been fooled for a minute, especially as Ireland wrote everything in the most ridiculous spelling – which is nothing like real Elizabethan spelling – and put double letters and extra e's on the end of every other word. Here is a little poem which, according to Ireland, Shakespeare wrote to Anne:

Is there onne earthe a manne more trew
Thanne Willy Shakespeare is toe you?

And here is a letter from Queen Elizabeth to Shakespeare, which reads:

We shalle departe fromme Londonne toe Hamptowne forre the hoyldayes where wee shall expecte thee with thye best Actorres thatte thou mayste playe before ourselfe to amuse usse.

For a time, people offered huge sums of money to buy these rubbishy olde documentes, but the ruse was soon rumbled. Today, two hundred years later, there is still a lot of puzzlement about various documents, papers and pictures. In 2001 an old gentleman in Canada presented an art gallery with a small painted portrait of an Elizabethan gentleman. On the back of the panel someone has written 'Shakespere: Born April 23 1564. Died April 23 1616. Aged 52. This likeness taken 1603. Age at that time 39 years.' The man in the painting has brownish hair and bluey eyes, and he certainly looks like a playwright or a poet. But there are also at least 400 other portraits said to be of Shakespeare, and nobody knows for sure whether any of them were genuinely painted from life – even the one that inspired the picture on the back of this book!

If you were interested in cryptograms and can be bothered to look back through this book, you would find that it's full of words like 'probably', 'maybe' and 'perhaps'. You see, this is what it come down to: we know there are these wonderful plays, which have thrilled people all over the world for four hundred years. They were probably written by someone called William Shakespeare who was born in Stratford-upon-Avon in 1564 – but beyond that, you have to write your own story. And your guess is as good as mine.

# <u>SHAKESPEARE STATISTICS</u>

# THE BARE FACTS

BORN 1564, STRATFORD-UPON AVON,
WARWICKSHIRE

MARRIED ANNE HATHAWAY, 1582

CHILDREN:
SUSANNA (BORN 1583);
HAMNET AND JUDITH (TWINS,
BORN 1585)

BOUGHT NEW PLACE,
STRATFORD-UPON-AVON, 1597

DIED 1616, STRATFORD–UPON-AVON

## SHAKESPEARE'S PLAYS IN THE ORDER THAT MOST HISTORIANS THINK THEY WERE WRITTEN

### 1590-1600

The Two Gentlemen of
Verona
The Taming of the Shrew
Henry VI part 2
Henry VI part 3
Henry VI part 1
Titus Andronicus
Richard III
The Comedy of Errors
Love's Labour's Lost
Richard II
A Midsummer Night's
Dream
King John
The Merchant of Venice
Henry IV part 1
The Merry Wives of
Windsor
Henry IV part 2
Much Ado about Nothing
Henry V
Julius Caesar

### 1600-1611

Hamlet
Twelfth Night
Troilus and Cressida
Measure for Measure
Othello
All's Well that Ends Well
Timon of Athens
King Lear
Macbeth
Antony and Cleopatra
Coriolanus
The Winter's Tale
Cymbeline
The Tempest

## PLAYS THAT SHAKESPEARE
### PROBABLY WROTE PART OF

Sir Thomas More
Pericles
Edward III
Henry VIII
The Two Noble Kinsmen

## THEATRES WHERE YOU CAN SEE
## SHAKESPEARE'S PLAYS PERFORMED

### Great Britain:
Royal Shakespeare Theatre, Waterside, Stratford-upon-Avon (April-November, 0870 6091110, www.rsc.org.uk)

Open Air Theatre, Regent's Park, London, NW1 (summer only, 020 7486 2431, www.open-air-theatre.org.uk)

Bankside Globe, Bankside, London SE1 (April-September, 020 7401 9919, www.shakespeares-globe.org)

### Canada:
The Stratford Festival, Stratford, Ontario (summer only, 800 567 12600, www.stratfordfestival.ca)

### United States of America:
Chicago Shakespeare Theatre, Navy Pier, Chicago, Illinois (312 595 5600, www.chicagoshakes.com)

## PLACES WHERE YOU CAN SEE
## RELICS OF SHAKESPEARE'S TIME

Shakespeare's Birthplace,
Anne Hathaway's Cottage,
New Place and Holy Trinity Church –
all in Stratford-upon-Avon
(01789 204016,
www.shakespeare–org.uk)

Bankside Globe,
Bankside,
London SE1
(020 7401 9919,
www.shakespeares-globe.org)

The Theatre Museum,
Covent Garden,
London WC2
(020 7836 7891,
www.theatremuseum.vam.ac.uk)

AND FINALLY, SOME CURSES AND INSULTS MADE
UP OF WORDS USED IN SHAKESPEARE'S TIME:

Thou dronking dog-hearted dewberry
Thou beslubbering clapper-clawed maggot-pie
Thou bootless tardy-gaited apple-john
Thou clouted hedge-born lout
Thou mangled flap-mouth
Thou impertinent beetle-headed hugger-mugger
Thou pribbling milk-livered pignut

Don't EVER use these in front of an adult!

Rupert Christiansen has written a number of books on music and history. He is a columnist for the *Daily Telegraph*. He lives in London, and goes to the theatre at least three times a week

Dear Reader,

No matter how old you are, good books always leave you wanting to know more. If you have any questions you would like to ask the author, **Rupert Christiansen,** about **William Shakespeare** please write to us at: SHORT BOOKS 15 Highbury Terrace, London N5 1UP.

If you enjoyed this title, then you would probably enjoy others in the series. Why not click on our website for more information and see what the teachers are being told? **www.theshortbookco.com**

All the books in the WHO WAS... series are available from TBS, Distribution Centre, Colchester Road, Frating Green, Colchester, Essex CO7 7DW (Tel: 01206 255800), at £4.99 + P&P.

**WHO WAS... Florence Nightingale**
**The Lady and the Lamp**
Charlotte Moore

Even as a little girl, Florence Nightingale knew she was different. Unlike the rest of her family, she wasn't interested in fancy clothes or grand parties. She knew God wanted her to do something different, something important... but what?

In 1854, shocking everyone, she set off to help save the thousands of British soldiers injured in the disastrous Crimean war. Nothing could have prepared her for the horror of the army hospital, where soldiers writhed in agony as rats scuttled around them on the blood-stained floor.

But Florence set to work, and became the greatest nurse the world had ever seen...

ISBN: 1-904095-83-6

WHO WAS... **Alexander Selkirk**
**Survivor on a Desert Island**
Amanda Mitchison

On the beach stood a wild thing waving its arms and hollering. The thing had the shape of a man, but it was all covered in fur, like a Barbary ape. What was it? A new kind of animal? A monster?

It was Alexander Selkirk, Scottish mariner and adventurer, thrilled to be rescued by passing sailors after four years alone on a Pacific island. This is the story of how Selkirk came to be stranded on the island and how he survived, the story of... THE REAL ROBINSON CRUSOE.

ISBN: 1-904095-79-8

WHO WAS... **Admiral Nelson**
**The Sailor Who Dared All to Win**
Sam Llewellyn

No one ever imagined that a weak skinny boy like Horatio Nelson would be able to survive the hardships of life at sea. But he did. In fact he grew up to become a great naval hero, the man who saved Britain from invasion by the dreaded Napoleon.

Nelson was someone who always did things his own way. He lost an eye and an arm in battle, but never let that hold him back. He was brilliant on ships, clumsy on land, ferocious in battle, knew fear but overcame it, and never, never took no for an answer.

This is his story.

ISBN: 1-904095-65-8

Charlotte Brontë
The girl who turned her life into a book
Kate Hubbard
1-904095-80-1

Ned Kelly
Gangster hero of the Australian outback
Charlie Boxer
1-904095-61-5

David Livingstone
The legendary explorer
Amanda Mitchison
1-904095-84-4

Madame Tussaud
Waxwork queen of the French Revolution
Tony Thorne
1-904095-85-2

Nelson Mandela
The prisoner who gave the world hope
Adrian Hadland
1-904095-86-0